DIGITAL AND INFORMATION LITERACY™

CREATING AND BUILDING YOUR OWN YOUTUBE CHANNEL

KEVIN HALL

rosen publishing's
rosen central®

New York

Published in 2017 by The Rosen Publishing Group, Inc.
29 East 21st Street, New York, NY 10010

Copyright © 2017 by The Rosen Publishing Group, Inc.

First Edition

Library of Congress Cataloging-in-Publication Data

Names: Hall, Kevin, 1990– author.
Title: Creating and building your own Youtube channel / Kevin Hall.
Description: First edition. | New York : Rosen Central, 2017. | Series: Digital and information literacy | Includes bibliographical references and index.
Identifiers: LCCN 2016017423| ISBN 9781508173281 (library bound) | ISBN 9781508173267 (pbk.) | ISBN 9781508173274 (6-pack)
Subjects: LCSH: YouTube (Firm) —Juvenile literature. | Internet videos—Juvenile literature. | Online social networks—Juvenile literature.
Classification: LCC TK5105.8868.Y68 H35 2017 | DDC 006.7—dc23
LC record available at https://lccn.loc.gov/2016017423

Manufactured in China

CONTENTS

INTRODUCTION

The internet is one of the most important tools of American life today. People of all ages rely on it for many purposes. They might look up the weather report or check up on current events. Perhaps instead they use it to find information for their businesses. Whatever the case, the internet has become endlessly useful. Several sites have made their mark both on the internet as well as American cultural life.

YouTube is one of today's top websites. In 2014, it became the second-largest search engine on the planet. Every minute, three hundred hours of video are uploaded to the site. It is clear that YouTube is a website that has made its mark on the world today. But what is YouTube? Why has it become one of the biggest websites on the internet?

In simple terms, YouTube is a website created for sharing videos. Before it was founded in 2005, posting a video online was a difficult task. It required large amounts of time and special equipment. Things are different today. With only a computer, millions of videos are uploaded and watched on YouTube every day. Clearly, many people flock to upload videos on this site for a reason.

YouTube channels are a key ingredient of what makes YouTube so powerful and successful. YouTube channels have helped both businesses and individuals grow and thrive. They have changed the way people view

This is a YouTube home screen. After clicking through this screen, you can see all the videos and features on the website.

videos. Before YouTube, the main source of video was via TV channels. Someone not watching could easily miss out. Now, anyone who wishes to watch a specific video can do so. They only have to type in "YouTube.com" to an internet browser, search for a particular video, and click play.

YouTube has quickly become the new platform for both entertainment and business. Content can be put up on the site by an individual trying to gain a fan base. Or a small business might use it to try and expand its product's reach. It is obvious that the website has made an impact on the world today. Many people have established their own YouTube channels and have become famous because of their channel's success. YouTube stars like PewDiePie and Vsauce have become wealthy and well-known based on the videos they post regularly.

Clearly, YouTube channels are an important part of the internet. However, they also serve purposes other than achieving fame and fortune. There are many ways in which teens can use YouTube channels for their own benefit. For example, they might create an online portfolio to enhance their résumés. Such an effort could strengthen college applications. Creating something that could be seen by (hopefully) millions of YouTube viewers creates endless possibilities. This book will explain the basics of YouTube so that you can create specific content for your own channel. You will also learn all you need to know about the various ways in which YouTube channels can help you grow and succeed.

Chapter 1

The Basics of YouTube and YouTube Channels

One key part of YouTube is located in its name. It is all about what you, the viewer, decide to watch. Once you log in and start watching videos, the website tracks your viewing habits. It also recommends similar videos to you. Once YouTube understands what content you enjoy, it will bring more of the same to you, the viewer. Once you log in and start watching videos, YouTube immediately starts trying to find videos based off your interests.

This ties back in with the main purpose of YouTube: watching videos. This, after all, is why so many

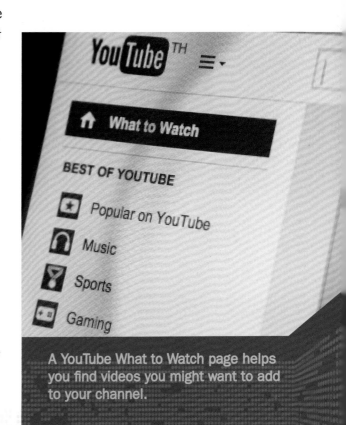

A YouTube What to Watch page helps you find videos you might want to add to your channel.

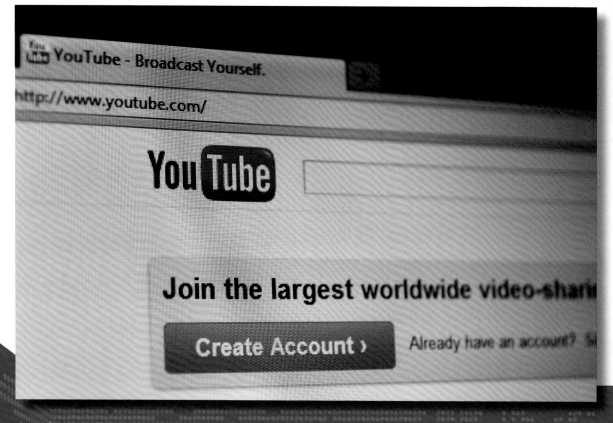

After you have viewed the What to Watch page, you can go ahead and create a YouTube account and get your channel going!

people visit the site. When you click on any video there, you'll be taken to a Watch page. The Watch page is for viewing videos, but it has a number of other purposes.

What's There to See?

Before you even create an account on YouTube, you can still search the various videos located there. The site has not yet had the chance to record your viewing history. Because of that, it cannot narrow down the content

File   Edit   View   Favorites   Tools   Help

YOUTUBE VERTICALS

YouTube Verticals

The YouTube verticals presented on the screen before you create an account are helpful. This feature is a way to figure out what you want your channel to contain. Your channel doesn't necessarily have to fall under one of these categories. But if you're not sure about what direction to go in, they can be very helpful.

Music is a popular category on YouTube. The site has pretty much replaced any music website for showing music videos. Sports videos are also very popular, ranging from those from known leagues like the NFL and NBA to amateur athletic games and stunts.

Other verticals such as gaming, movies, and education can also serve as inspiration before you and your channel truly take off. YouTube verticals are a good way to understand what people on the site search for. Again, your channel doesn't have to fall into one of these categories. However, it is a good place to start.

of the videos you search for. At first, then, you are presented with various choices based on what is trending and popular. On the left side of the screen you will see a list of The Best of YouTube channels. These categories are known as verticals. They're the way YouTube divides the many videos found on its website.

What's Not There to See?

In terms of the verticals, it is clear that there is already a set range of topics covered on YouTube. There are certain topics that are not allowed

Uploading hateful, violent, or stolen material can lead to serious trouble. Make sure your video content is safe for all to see.

on YouTube as well. Be sure not to upload anything that violates these guidelines. If you do, you won't have to worry about maintaining your channel. This is because you won't have an account to start with. YouTube will shut it down. Extreme violence, hate speech, illegal actions, and stolen material can all lead to you losing your account. Be sure to read YouTube's community guidelines. They can help guide you as you create videos and build your channel.

Creating an Account

One of the most important things to do before searching for the millions of videos on YouTube is to create an account. Although this isn't necessary for browsing, it is in order to create a YouTube channel. After you create an account, you will be free to shoot and upload videos for your channel. One key thing to remember here is that when you sign up for a YouTube account, you are also signing up for a Google account. Google owns YouTube. They have been trying to unite all their products under one log-in. With one username and password, you can gain access to both the YouTube and Gmail platforms.

Once you have a valid Google account, it is quite easy to set up a YouTube channel. First you must enter http://www.youtube.com into your internet browser. The main YouTube home screen will appear. In the upper right corner of the home page, your account profile picture is shown. If you click on it, you will go to the Google account menu. This will also be featured on the top right corner of the screen.

To continue, click on the My Channel link. This will be on the upper right corner of the screen. Now a screen saying "Create Your YouTube channel" will be shown. This screen will show your profile photo, as well as the username you've chosen after making your YouTube account.

Now that you've created an account, you are free to explore the huge number of videos on YouTube. Each and every video has a video info screen.

You create a Google account when you sign up for a YouTube account. This account can also assist you as you develop your YouTube channel.

There are many important things to look at in this screen. One is the title. Titles provide valuable information in your YouTube channel. They give your viewers an idea of what your content is about. Underneath the title is information about your channel. This includes the name of the channel as well as a logo, also known as the channel icon. Another important feature is the like or dislike option. These are also known as the thumbs-up and thumbs-down buttons. This feature helps to build an audience for your channel. Knowing how your audience feels about your video helps you to

What's in a Name?

Before you create a video, you must choose a name for your channel. This is one of the most important things you can do for it. Take your time before settling on a name. Here are some tips to help you choose the best name for your channel.

- Make it relates to your channel. If your channel is about college football, make sure the channel name is related to college football.

- Avoid obscene language. You want people to subscribe and ultimately share your videos. If you use profane language, you'll limit your audience. Some people are offended by such language, and some young people may have this content screened by their parents.

- Make sure the name is available. If the name of your channel is too close to another one, people will get confused. They might subscribe to the wrong channel. Make sure you are concise and your name is easy to find. After all, you want your channel to take off.

maintain and change your channel for the better. Finally, there is a share option. This is a useful tool for your audience. People can use it to share your videos, which enables you to gain a wider audience.

Now that you have an account and have completed the basic setup for a channel, you're well on your way to creating a presence on YouTube. This chapter has given you the basic information about what

YouTube is. It has also covered the first steps needed to create both an account and a channel.

Next you can create your channel by deciding what videos to shoot and upload. YouTube has two main uses. Most users watch videos on it. Once you log in, every YouTube viewer will be met with many videos to choose from. This allows people to watch, or consume, content. The other main use is to create and share content. After you create your channel, you will want to build upon it. Remember, the videos you choose to upload to YouTube are your channel's main attraction. But making your channel look good is important, too. Fortunately, YouTube provides its users with many tools that enhance their channels. In the next chapters, you will learn how to do just that.

Chapter 2

Creating and Building Your Channel

You've survived your basic YouTube crash course! You are now on your way to creating your channel. You must keep one thing in mind before you do this: content. Content is another word for subject matter. Basically, it is what your YouTube channel will show.

Content Is Key

But before creating your channel, you need to know why you're creating one in the first place. Are you using it to tell a story? Are you trying to market a business or product? Are you looking to showcase your creative skills? Whatever your reason, it is important to keep it in mind. If you don't have a clear goal before you create your channel, you'll run into problems when you start shooting videos. Remember the YouTube verticals discussed earlier? Go back and look over those if you're still not sure what you want your channel to focus on.

When building your channel, you should think about how to structure it. This is true whether your channel is geared toward business or entertainment. Everyone with a YouTube channel must make sure it is clear and easy to follow. One key thing to keep in mind is the content of your videos. For example, let's say that your channel is used to promote a product. In that case, make sure all the videos on your channel are about that product. What happens if you add a video that has nothing to do with the content of your channel? Your subscribers may become confused and the quality of your channel will suffer. Only upload videos that relate to the overall theme of your channel.

It is important that the videos on your channel are clear to your audience. Engaging and keeping your audience will be covered more in the next chapter. An important part of any YouTube channel is consistency. You have to establish a regular schedule in terms of when you post videos to

Think of your YouTube channel as your personal business. It is your responsibility to maintain it and make people interested in your product.

your channel. Whether you post once a week, three times a month, or every other day, you will need to make a schedule and then keep to it. This draws people to tune into your channel regularly. Sticking to a schedule proves to your viewers that you're passionate and serious about your efforts.

You may be wondering what equipment is needed to upload videos. Many popular YouTube channels have loads of cameras and other equipment to help them shoot video. However, if you have a smartphone, you're already well on your way. The camera quality on smartphones is good enough to start shooting video. You can always upgrade what you're using as you develop your channel. Keep in mind that your audience won't be showing up just to see how fancy your equipment is. This leads to the vital part of building your channel: videos.

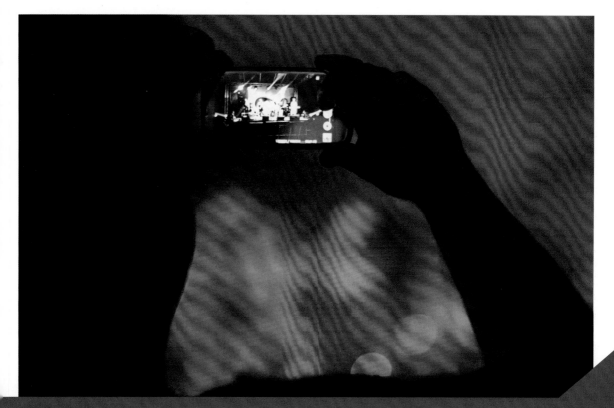

Keep your videos simple when starting out. A smartphone is a useful tool for capturing and editing videos for your channel.

Don't complicate your videos with complex special effects or graphics. The message should be clear and understandable to those viewing it. There are certain elements every successful video on your channel should have.

The Introduction

The very beginning of the video should serve one purpose. It should tell the viewer what your video is about. This is crucial, as it lets viewers know what they are seeing. It also shows that you have a clear goal in mind with the videos you create. You can include a title sequence and the contributors here. But keep in mind that this should be a small part of your video (no more than a minute in most cases).

The Subject

This is where your video kicks into high gear. Whereas your introduction should not be too long, here you can slow down and take your time with the video. Depending on the subject, you should take all the time you need to make what you present to your viewers clear, helpful, and, fun, if that's what you are going for.

The End

The end of your video should have similar information to the beginning. One thing many people do is to thank their viewers for watching their video. Make sure the end wraps up your content. Another tip is to provide links for similar videos. This will help your viewers see other content they might find interesting.

Review and Move Forward

Congratulations! You have figured out the type of channel you want. You've also made a video. What's next? You're ready to upload it to your channel.

Cyberbullying has become a huge problem for teens and parents today. Avoid personal attacks in your videos. Be helpful, not hateful.

Be sure that you use YouTube's tools to upload your finished video file to your account. You can upload video from your smartphone, your computer, your camera, or your video camera.

The title of your video is very important in terms of gaining viewers for your channel. We've already covered having a consistent schedule for putting out videos. Your titles should follow a model like this, too. Don't mislead your viewers. If your channel is about tacos, make sure your title has something to do with tacos. Be clear. Your viewers will thank you for it.

Pay attention to the message your videos are sending. They should not attack other people. In our society today, cyberbullying has become a common problem. Many people use the internet as a means of attacking others. Make sure that your channel spreads a message that is worthy, not one that encourages hatred of any kind.

Many young people use YouTube. Some of them have their own channels. Because of this, YouTube has included tips and ways to combat

File   Edit   View   Favorites   Tools   Help

WHAT IS CYBERBULLYING?

What Is Cyberbullying?

According to the Cyberbullying Research Center, cyberbullying is "willful and repeated harm inflicted through the use of computers, cell phones, and other electronic devices." Simply put, cyberbullying is a form of bullying done with electronic technology. People who engage in this behavior are known as cyberbullies. Cyberbullying is different from regular bullying. This is because those who engage in it are doing it over the internet instead of face-to-face. This distance can keep people from behaving politely because they do not think they will get caught. Don't risk it, though. A good rule of thumb is this: if you wouldn't say it to your mother, don't say it at all.

cyberbullying. Take a look at the site's privacy and safety settings page. There, you will see a number of ways to deal with people who harass or abuse you through the site. Someone could put up a video that personally attacks you. Or it could be that someone keeps posting negative comments on your videos. YouTube has policies set in place to help you combat constant harassment.

Keep in mind that YouTube is a social platform. Just like in everyday life, not everyone agrees on everything. However, that does not mean people need to be humiliated or abused for having a different opinion. YouTube works to prevent and stop cyberbullying whenever it can. You can also help out by regulating your own channel to protect against harassment. Your YouTube channel should focus on your passions and interests. It should not become a forum for hate, anger, or crudity.

Now that you have a channel and videos to upload, you're well on your way to setting up a great YouTube channel. However, your journey is far from over. Sure, you already have a lot of the things needed to make your impact on YouTube: a channel theme, equipment, and videos. But there's more that you need. We've focused already on the "you" part of YouTube. What about the people that you want to watch your videos? They are a necessary part of your channel!

MYTHS & FACTS

MYTH *Your YouTube channel will be an overnight success.*

FACT There is something on YouTube and the larger internet known as the viral video. This is when a video becomes hugely popular. It gets this way due to video sharing through social media and email. However, for every video that goes viral, there are thousands that don't. Building a successful YouTube channel takes time.

MYTH *You can use another person's content on your video channel without permission.*

FACT You can get into trouble for not asking to use other people's content. You're violating that person's copyright, which is a serious matter. Your channel can be shut down if you do this. Ask for permission every time.

MYTH *It is okay to harass and criticize other people's videos on YouTube.*

FACT Cyberbullying is a real problem today. Although you may not like someone's video or agree with the ideas expressed in it, it is that person's right to post it. Criticizing people on YouTube won't accomplish anything. In fact, it will probably make you feel bad afterward.

Chapter 3

Building Your Channel's Audience

You've put in a lot of hard work with your YouTube channel. You've decided what type of videos you're going to show. You've designed the channel in a way that's interesting and engaging. You've even recorded your first video or two. What's next? You have to get your content out to an audience that will enjoy your work. There are many ways you can attract people to watch your videos and subscribe to your channel.

Who Sees Your Work?

No matter how big or small, an audience is a crucial part of the success of any YouTube channel. This audience could be coming to your channel for many different reasons. Such reasons could include entertainment, instruction, or just curiosity. You will undoubtedly want to know how to build up traffic, or the number of viewers you get. There are different techniques you can use to accomplish this.

You must make sure your channel is focused on drawing an audience. Your videos may be great, but that means nothing if nobody sees them.

As big as you want your channel to be, it is important to keep in mind that building an audience takes time. YouTube celebrities spend a lot of effort and time developing their channels and building audiences. There is a single, simple method to ensure that people tune in and subscribe to the videos on your channel. You have to make videos that people want to watch. Don't just make two or three videos and give up if no one subscribes to your channel.

Linking to Your Videos on Other Websites

Many people with YouTube channels also have accounts on social media sites like Twitter and Instagram. Consider how you can use these sites to promote your YouTube channel. Perhaps you want to post your video to your personal Facebook account or to a Twitter page dedicated to your channel.

(continued on the next page)

You can use social media sites like Instagram to promote your channel's content. These sites are helpful tools. Don't be afraid to use them!

(continued from the previous page)

Whatever you choose to do, you have many tools at your disposal that will help you broaden your audience. Having a YouTube channel is the most obvious way to spread your videos. But using other social media accounts can help you expand your reach.

Building and maintaining an audience for your YouTube channel is about making sure people watch your videos and engaging with them.

A lot of what you need to do to ensure the success of your YouTube channel happens outside of YouTube. One thing to have is a website. You have complete control over your website. No matter how simple or ambitious you want to be with your YouTube channel, having a website is crucial. The site allows your viewers to become more involved with the subjects revolving around your channel. Your website can be used to post updates about your channel. This keeps your audience interested in you and your content.

YouTube is a huge online community. The thing that links every user on the website is their interests. People come to YouTube to find videos about topics they want to explore further. Whether they enjoy exotic cuisine, Lady Gaga, or football, many people come to YouTube to find videos about things they are passionate about. This leads to a chain of events that will help you engage and maintain an audience for your channel.

Let's say your channel is about football. A viewer will come across one of your videos. Impressed or entertained by what they saw, they then visit your channel to look at more of your videos. A channel that is properly designed and organized may convince them to keep looking at your videos. Hopefully, they end up subscribing to your channel. This will allow them to access new videos and other relevant news.

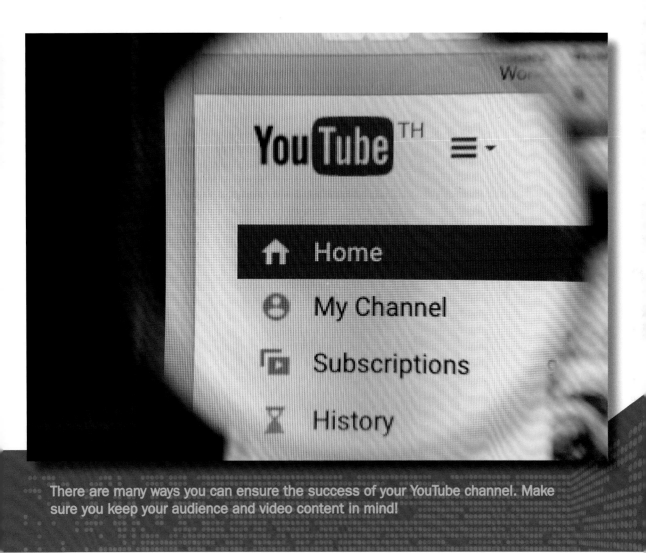

There are many ways you can ensure the success of your YouTube channel. Make sure you keep your audience and video content in mind!

One key way of promoting your own channel as well as engaging with your audience is using social media. YouTube is just one of the many social media sites on the internet today. Facebook, Instagram, and Twitter are other examples of social media sites. They can also be used to promote your channel and interact with your audience. Posting links to your videos on these sites can gain you a wider audience, as people on these sites will now know about your YouTube channel.

Ways to Engage with Your Viewers

Another way to engage with your audience is through email lists. Compiling an email list of your subscribers may seem like a difficult task. However, it is worth it, as you will have another way to contact all of the people who watch your videos. The emails you send don't have to be complicated. Simple messages, delivered either weekly or biweekly, are effective ways of maintaining an audience.

A lot of ways to build an audience have nothing to do with the videos themselves. They're more about building your channel. However, a great channel must also have great videos. Viral videos were mentioned in chapter two. Viral videos are good for a growing channel, but it is important to realize that not every video becomes viral. There are ways,

File   Edit   View   Favorites   Tools   Help

VIDCON

VidCon

If live hangouts or vlogs aren't doing enough to enhance your channel, there is another option. Held every year in Anaheim, California, VidCon is a three-day conference at which video creators and fans gather. It is for those with an established YouTube channel with millions of subscribers and those just getting their feet in the door. There, you can attend meetups or panel discussions on subjects that interest you. You can get autographs from online celebrities. If that's not enough, there's a well-attended Expo Hall, in which attendees showcase their online products and personalities.

All in all, VidCon is a great way for people with YouTube channels to come together to learn more about their beloved online community.

however, to ensure the videos you upload keep your audience coming back for more.

When people are looking for a video on YouTube, they often have a specific idea in mind. If they're searching for a video about a certain type of food, they enter that food in the search box. This ties in with your channel because of a concept known as keywords. Keywords are words or phrases that people type into a search engine to find out information. Many words and phrases get entered a lot. These become popular keywords. If one of your videos pops up after a popular keyword is entered, it may help your video gain popularity. This ties in with a concept called search engine

VidCon is a yearly conference where many people with YouTube channels can learn ways to enhance their content and presence on the website.

optimization, also known as SEO. This is the method of increasing the number of visitors to a certain site or channel. It is done by ensuring that the site or channel appears high in a list of results returned by a search engine.

The relationship between a YouTube channel and a subscriber is a two-way street. If viewers enjoy the video, they can show it by liking the video. But that isn't the only thing they can do. They can also leave comments on the video to show their support. They can engage with other channel subscribers by having conversations in the comments sections of your videos. You also should remember that you must remain active on YouTube. Be a part of the conversation, whether it's on your own video or a similar one. Your viewers will see that you care and are engaged. That will help convince them to subscribe to your videos. The relationship you have with your subscribers is vital.

One way to connect with your audience is through vlogs. Vlogs are simple videos that allow your audience to gain access to a part of you that you don't normally show in your videos. Similar to vlogs are Q&A videos, in which those with YouTube channels answer questions from their subscribers. This is a good way for you to interact with your audience and allow them access into your world. Another way to engage with fans is by setting up live hangouts. You can invite your fans to an event and stream it live so other fans can see.

Building and maintaining an audience for your channel is hard work. But it can be worth it. By creating engaging content and interacting with your fans, over time you can establish your channel. If you keep at it and luck comes your way, there's no limit to how huge your channel can be.

Chapter 4

The Personal Benefits of Having a YouTube Channel

We've discussed some of the various celebrities who achieved fame through their YouTube channels. They are good examples of how having a YouTube channel can benefit a person. Still, it is important to understand that there are countless others who aren't looking to achieve the same things as people like PewDiePie. There are many ways in which YouTube has made an impact on the world. Many channels on the site are dedicated to serving people's needs. YouTube can be used to launch a career or gain someone fame and fortune. It can be used for other purposes as well.

Education and YouTube

One area that has become associated with the popularity of YouTube channels is education. Many teachers and students use YouTube channels for their own purposes. For example, teachers might use videos for their own lesson plans. Or a student might use videos to complete an assignment or test. It's official. YouTube has entered the classroom. One example of a

YouTube videos and tutorials are useful ways for students and teachers to learn something about a new subject.

channel used for educational purposes is Vsauce. Vsauce is a YouTube channel about math and science. It has more than ten million subscribers and almost one billion total views. While these numbers are common for YouTube stars, it is truly impressive for a channel dedicated to educational content. With videos like "What if the Earth Stopped Spinning?" and "Is Your Red the Same as My Red?," this channel, created by Michael Stevens, has made its mark on YouTube as an educational video powerhouse. Vsauce videos combine educational content with entertaining visuals and easy-to-follow instruction.

File   Edit   View   Favorites   Tools   Help

ORIGINALITY AND COPYRIGHT

Originality and Copyright

No matter what the subject matter of your channel's videos, you must keep one thing in mind: originality. YouTube tries to present itself as a site where people can post their own original content. However, the site has had problems with protecting copyright. Copyright is the exclusive legal right granted by law to protect owners of original works. The creator of a particular video has the copyright to the video. This means they can use the video for their own specific purposes. It is important that your videos do not copy other people's work. If they do, you will be accused of plagiarism. This is the act of taking someone else's work and passing it off as your own. Not only will you not be able to maintain a YouTube channel, you may also face legal action. If you wish to include someone else's work, such as a song or video, you must ask for permission before doing it.

Vsauce has established itself as a prominent channel. But that doesn't mean you can't create your own channel to use either for school projects or to help your teachers with lesson plans. YouTube is banned in many schools, as many teachers and administrators believe students will use it to look at videos that have no bearing on their education. However, YouTube can be used as a learning tool.

Instead of assigning traditional outlines and research reports, a teacher can ask students to create YouTube channels for certain classes. Teachers can monitor progress by asking their students to update their channels. These updates might be about certain assignments or the videos might serve

Be careful that you have the rights you need when recording performances. Otherwise you can face serious legal trouble and have your channel shut down.

as assignments themselves. These channels will likely not launch anyone into huge internet fame. They are a way to use a YouTube channel for personal benefit.

Who Sees You Online

We have already talked about avoiding vulgarity and profane language in your videos. Such elements often drive people away from your content.

However, there is another reason why you should monitor your presence on YouTube and other forms of social media. When you begin applying for college, those in charge of acceptances may check your online presence. If your content on a YouTube channel or anywhere else is full of inappropriate material and bad language, you may find that you are passed over. The same is true when you look for a job. Colleges and employers want to be careful about who represents them to the outside world. Be careful. A video that you created years back may haunt you later.

Videos you create for school assignments can be used outside of the classroom as well. Many colleges have started accepting application videos from prospective students. Tufts University, in Massachusetts, has been accepting YouTube videos as a part of their applications since 2010. These video essays usually follow a prompt. Students have a limited amount of time to talk about their knowledge and abilities. So no matter if you're completing a high school project or trying to continue your education outside of high school, a YouTube channel can help you along the way.

Employment and YouTube

YouTube channels can have a profound impact in the classroom. They can help you in other ways as well. Just as modern technology has changed the classroom, it has changed the working world as well. Many job applications ask for a video from the applicant. Similar to Tufts and its process, the purpose of the video is to demonstrate why the applicant is worthy of the position. This is another reason why having a YouTube channel could come in handy.

On your channel, you can show how you have the skills needed for a specific job. All jobs list the skills and requirements necessary in order to do that job effectively. In your application, it is easy to say that you are skilled in the things the job is calling for. However, if you create a YouTube channel dedicated to showing your job skills, you might stand apart from the crowd. Many people would not put forth the effort to create one video much less a

You can create an online portfolio using YouTube videos. This may help you gain an edge in a competitive job market.

whole channel. It is easy to say you can do certain tasks. But showing that you can do those tasks on a video is a much stronger statement. It proves to prospective employers that your skills are legitimate. This could give you a leg up over others applying for the job you want.

Another way a YouTube channel can help you is to allow you to gain fans. Perhaps you have a specific set of skills you wish to teach to others. You can do this on your YouTube channel. This can bring you to the attention of potential employers. If your video becomes popular, you may be

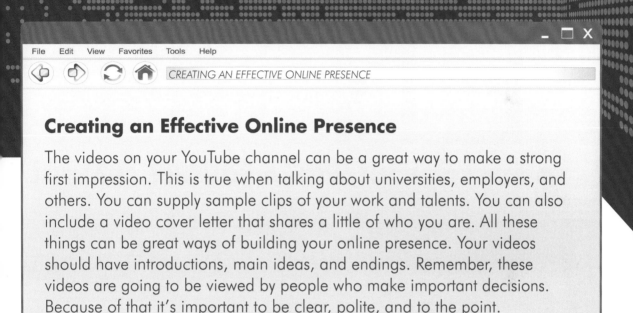

File   Edit   View   Favorites   Tools   Help

CREATING AN EFFECTIVE ONLINE PRESENCE

Creating an Effective Online Presence

The videos on your YouTube channel can be a great way to make a strong first impression. This is true when talking about universities, employers, and others. You can supply sample clips of your work and talents. You can also include a video cover letter that shares a little of who you are. All these things can be great ways of building your online presence. Your videos should have introductions, main ideas, and endings. Remember, these videos are going to be viewed by people who make important decisions. Because of that it's important to be clear, polite, and to the point.

asked to speak at certain events related to your skill set. Keep in mind that the ways you engage your channel audience are important. First impressions make a big difference. You must make sure your videos, like the ones you promote to your channel audience, are clear and appropriate, depending on your viewers.

YouTube channels have launched the careers of many celebrities. They've garnered many followers that helped them make their way into popular culture. While YouTube can lead to such a career, it also serves many practical purposes. Whether it's a channel dedicated to highlighting your academic talents or showing your skills for the working world, it can work wonders in your own life. There's no telling how YouTube will factor into the future as the technology progresses and improves. But it is clear that YouTube channels have a direct impact on lives today.

TEN GREAT QUESTIONS

TO ASK SOMEONE WITH A YOUTUBE CHANNEL

1 What is your channel about?

2 How long have you been on YouTube?

3 How do you engage with your audience?

4 What's the most rewarding thing about having a channel?

5 Have you ever had problems with trolling or cyberbullying?

6 Do you think YouTube can do anything to improve their channels?

7 What is your favorite channel?

8 What goals do you have for your channel?

9 If you could give one piece of advice for people wanting to start a channel, what would it be?

10 How has having a YouTube channel changed your life?

GLOSSARY

content The subject matter of your YouTube video.

copyright The exclusive legal right granted by law to protect owners of original works.

cyberbullying Bullying done with electronic technology.

email lists List of emails of people who subscribe to your channel.

keywords Words or phrases typed into a search engine when people are researching information.

plagiarism The act of stealing someone else's work and claiming it as one's own.

promotion The practice of actively raising awareness about a channel.

search engine An online site designed to search for information on the internet.

search engine optimization The act of maximizing the amount of visitors to a particular site or video by making sure the site or video appears high on the list of results returned by a search engine.

social media Applications and websites that allow users to create and share content and engage in networking.

traffic A term for the amount of viewers who visit a website or watch a YouTube channel.

troll A term for people who harass others on the internet.

verticals The primary ways content is divided on YouTube. Examples include gaming, education, and sports.

video essay A video usually sent to a college or employer that demonstrates an ability or talent.

viral video A video that gains fame through online sharing.

vlogs Videos you can post on your channel to give your audience more information about you. Short for video logs.

FOR MORE INFORMATION

Children's Safety Association of Canada
2110 Kipling Avenue
PO Box 551
Etobicoke, ON M9W 4KO
Canada
(888) 499-4444
Website: http://www.safekid.org/en
This is a non-profit Canadian organization that provides health and safety
    information including tips about online safety.

Cyberbullying Research Center
Email: Sameer Jinduja, Ph.D., hinduja@cyberbullying.org
Email: Justin W. Patchin, Ph.D., patchin@cyberbullying.org
Website: http://cyberbullying.org
This website contains stories about the recent trend of cyberbullying and
    provides parents and children useful ways of preventing and stopping it.

Family Online Safety Center
400 7th Street NW, Suite 506
    Washington, DC 20004
(202) 775-0158
Website: https://www.fosi.org/
The Family Online Safety Center stresses effective parenting as a way of
    promoting and maintaining online safety.

Imagine Canada
65 St Clair Ave E #700
Toronto, ON M4T 273 Canada
(800) 263-1178

Website: http://www.imaginecanada.ca
Imagine Canada works side by side with various charities and uses an
    ethical code to help run its operations.

Pixability
77 N Washington Street
Boston, MA 02114
(888) PIX-VIDEO (888-749-8433)
Website: www.pixability.com
This company uses the latest technology to create video advertising for
    YouTube, Twitter, and other social media platforms.

Websites

Because of the changing nature of internet links, Rosen Publishing has
developed an online list of websites related to the subject of this book. This
site is updated regularly. Please use this link to access this list:

http://www.rosenlinks.com/DIL/Youtu

FOR FURTHER READING

Besley, Adrian. *The Most Awesome YouTube Videos Ever! 150 of the Coolest, Craziest, and Funniest Internet Clips*. London: UK Carlton Books, 2014.

Burgess, Jean. *YouTube: Online Video and Participatory Culture*. 2nd ed. Cambridge, UK: Polity Press, 2016.

Davenport, Michelle. *The YouTube Manifesto: A Collection of the Top 5 Channels for Every Category Under the Sun*. Vol. 1. North Charleston, SC: CreateSpace Independent Publishing, 2015.

Ezarik, Justine. *I, Justine: An Analog Memoir*. New York, NY: Atria/Keywords Press, 2015.

Jackson, Martina. *YouTube Channel Behind the Scenes: All Your Questions Answered About Starting a YouTube Channel in This Book*. North Charleston, SC: CreateSpace Independent Publishing, 2015.

Jarboe, Greg. *YouTube and Video Marketing: An Hour a Day*. Hoboken, NJ: Sybex, 2011.

Joyner, Joseph. *YouTube for Beginners: Learn the Basics of YouTube, Get More Views, Likes, Attract New Subscribers, Earn Money Secrets Guide*. Newark, DE: Speedy Publishing LLC, 2015.

Lange, Patricia G. *Kids on YouTube: Technical Identities and Digital Literacies*. New York, NY: Routledge, 2014.

McAllister, Jenn. *Really Professional Internet Person*. New York, NY: Scholastic, 2015.

Miles, Jason G. *YouTube Marketing Power: How to Use Video to Find More Prospects, Launch Your Products, and Reach a Massive Audience*. New York, NY: McGraw-Hill Education, 2013.

Myers, Greg F. *YouTube for Beginners: The Complete Guide for Marketing Techniques, Audience Building, and Audience Retention*. North Charleston, SC: CreateSpace Independent Publishing, 2015.

Qualman, Erik. *What Happens on Campus Stays on YouTube*. Austin, TX: Equalman Studios, 2015.

Sales, Nancy Jo. *American Girls: Social Media and the Secret Lives of Teenagers*. New York, NY: Knopf, 2016.

Unsworth, Nick. *The Book on YouTube Marketing: To Help You Set Your Business and Life on Fire*. Carlsbad, CA: Crescendo Publishing, LLC, 2014.

Walter, Ekaterina, and Jessica Gioglio. *The Power of Visual Storytelling: How to Use Visuals, Videos, and Social Media to Market Your Brand*. New York, NY: McGraw-Hill Education, 2015.

Ciampa, Rob, Theresa Moore, John Carucci, Stan Muller, and Adam Wescott. *YouTube Channels for Dummies*. Hoboken, NJ: Wiley, 2015.

Fahs, Chad. *How to Do Everything with YouTube*. New York, NY: McGraw-Hill, 2008.

Kawasaki, Guy, and Peg Fitzpatrick. *The Art of Social Media: Power Tips for Power Users*. New York, NY: Portfolio, 2014.

Lastufka, Alan, and Michael W. Dean. *YouTube: An Insider's Guide to Climbing the Charts*. Beijing, CN: O'Reilly, 2009.

McKinnon, Andrew. *YouTube: Ultimate YouTube Guide to Building a Channel, Audience and to Start Making Passive Income*. North Charleston, SC: CreateSpace Independent, 2015.

Miles, Jay. *Conquering YouTube: 101 Pro Video Tips to Take You to the Top*. Studio City, CA: Michael Wiese Productions, 2011.

Miller, Michael. *YouTube 4 You*. Indianapolis, IN: Que, 2007.

Portis, Montina. *YouTube Video Marketing Secrets Revealed: The Beginners Guide to Online Video Marketing*. Roswell, GA: Creative Internet Authority, LLC, 2014.

Puchkov, Sergey. *YouTube Marketing: How to Create a Successful Channel and Make Money*. North Charleston, SC: CreateSpace Independent, 2016.

Stockman, Steve. *How to Shoot Video That Doesn't Suck*. New York, NY: Workman Publishing, 2011.

Zimmerman, Jan, and Deborah Ng. *Social Media Marketing All-in-One for Dummies*. Hoboken, NJ: Wiley, 2013.

INDEX

About The Author

Kevin Hall has used YouTube for various purposes, including school projects and components for job applications. While he does not have his own channel (yet), he has many friends who upload videos and use YouTube for their own purposes. He is a huge opponent of cyberbullying and does his best to avoid trolls at all costs. He is curious to see how YouTube will change and develop over the coming years. Kevin would like to thank Jeric Brual for his help with this book.

Photo Credits

Cover, p. 1 (left to right) Netfalls - Remy Musser/Shutterstock.com, cristovao/Shutterstock.com, kentoh/Shutterstock.com, Maxim Tarasyugin/Shutterstock.com; p. 5 Alexey Boldin/Shutterstock.com; p. 7 10 FACE/Shutterstock.com; p. 8 Annette Shaff/Shutterstock.com; p. 10 Sakdawut Tangtongsap/Shutterstock.com; p. 12 Aleksandra Gigowska/Shutterstock.com; p. 16 Iakov Filimonov/Shutterstock.com; p. 17 Ema Woo/Shutterstock.com; p. 19 SpeedKingz/Shutterstock.com; p. 24 Rawpixel.com/Shutterstock.com; p. 25 Ingvar Bjork/Shutterstock.com; p. 27 GongTo/Shutterstock.com; p. 29 Randy Miramontez/Shutterstock.com; p. 32 Andrey_Popov/Shutterstock.com; p. 34 © National Geographic Creative/Alamy Stock Photo; p. 36 © iStockphoto.com/sturti; cover and interior pages (pixels) © iStockphoto.com/suprun.

Designer: Nicole Russo; Editor: Xina M. Uhl; Photo Researcher: Xina M. Uhl